For all the brilliant Black girls who can now envision having a seat at the table —C.B.W.

For Auntie Janice. Thanks for always uplifting me. —A.E.

Text copyright © 2023 by Carole Boston Weatherford
Jacket art and interior illustrations copyright © 2023 by Ashley Evans

All rights reserved. Published in the United States by Crown Books for Young Readers, an imprint of Random House Children's Books, a division of Penguin Random House LLC, New York.

Crown and the colophon are registered trademarks of Penguin Random House LLC.

Visit us on the Web! rhcbooks.com

Educators and librarians, for a variety of teaching tools, visit us at RHTeachersLibrarians.com

Library of Congress Cataloging-in-Publication Data is available upon request.
ISBN 978-0-593-65016-5 (hardcover) — ISBN 978-0-593-65017-2 (lib. bdg.) — ISBN 978-0-593-65018-9 (ebook)

The text of this book is set in 15-point Adobe Caslon Pro semibold.
The illustrations in this book were created digitally with Photoshop and a Wacom Cintiq.
MANUFACTURED IN CHINA
10 9 8 7 6 5 4 3
First Edition

ALL RISE

The Story of Ketanji Brown Jackson

By **Carole Boston Weatherford** ★ Illustrated by **Ashley Evans**

Crown Books for Young Readers ♛ New York

Whatever she did, wherever she was,
Ketanji Brown Jackson rose to the top.

She rose

on the hopes of grandparents who only finished grade school
but instilled in Ketanji's parents the value of learning.

She rose

from the dedication and determination of her parents
who were the first in their families to go to college.

She rose

from her parents' pride in their heritage
that inspired her African name, Ketanji Onyika,
meaning "Lovely One."

And on the birthday of Constance Baker Motley,
the nation's first Black female federal judge,

Ketanji rose

to breathe her first breath, take her first glimpse,
and cry her first cry.

Wearing Afro puffs and an African dashiki,
she rose
from the Civil Rights Movement that pushed open doors
in the decade before her birth.

The gains of the movement
gave her parents hope that the way would be easier
for Ketanji and her little brother, Ketajh.

"My parents set out to teach me that . . . if I worked hard
and believed in myself, I could do anything
or be anything I wanted to be," she said.

Ketanji rose

from her family's dining room table, where she sat coloring while her father studied his law school textbooks.

She rose

above her family's sadness for an uncle who was in jail on drug charges.

She barely knew him beyond his occasional phone calls.
But she learned that there was a right and a wrong side of the law.

Ketanji rose

among her peers to be elected mayor
of Palmetto Junior High School
and three-time president
of Miami Palmetto Senior High School.

She rose

above the slight when a teacher would not cast her
as a family member in a play . . . because she was not white.

Ketanji rose

from acting and singing to conquering the debate stage, where she won national awards for public speaking.

Debate Team

Under the wing of her debate coach, Mrs. Fran Berger, Ketanji thrived.

"Mrs. Berger believed in me, and, in turn, I believed in myself."

Ketanji

She rose

above the debate judges who mocked her African name.
She'd respond by saying it clearly and writing it on the board:
K-e-t-a-n-j-i.

She rose

above a guidance counselor's doubts that she could get into Harvard, whose campus she had first visited for a speech competition. Instead of lowering her goals, Ketanji vowed, "I'll show them."

Brooks

Ketanji Onyika Brown

Ke

Ketanji rose

above her high school classmates to be named in the yearbook
as "most talented" and "most likely to succeed."
In that same yearbook, she mapped out her future:
"I want to go into law and eventually have a judicial
appointment."

Once at Harvard,

Ketanji rose

above lonely days as a first-year college student
thanks to her mother's birthday greeting and a
stranger's advice to "persevere."

With a diverse group of friends, she acted in plays—
even writing one—and joined in student protests.
But she always put her studies first.

Ketanji rose

from a Harvard College honor graduate
and a reporter for *Time* magazine to a Harvard Law student
and an editor of the school's prestigious law journal.

She rose

from the examples of service set by her mother, a school principal;
her father, a school board lawyer; and her uncles, both police officers.

She rose

to clerk for judges and to work as a public defender,
representing people who could not afford to pay for a lawyer.

And finally, **Ketanji rose**
to reach her goal of becoming a federal judge.
But she did not stop there.

She rose

to become an inspiration for her own two daughters.
Her youngest, Leila, wrote a letter urging President Barack Obama
to nominate her to the U.S. Supreme Court.
But the timing was not right. Not yet.

Then, six years later, President Joe Biden nominated Judge Ketanji Brown Jackson as an associate justice, calling her "one of the brightest legal minds."

At the announcement,
she rose
to give thanks:
"My life has been blessed beyond measure and I do know that one can only come this far by faith."

In four days of Senate Judiciary Committee hearings,

she rose

above tough questions, kept her calm, and stood her ground.

"I have dedicated my career to ensuring that the words engraved on the front of the Supreme Court building—'Equal Justice Under Law'—are a reality and not just an ideal."

As Vice President Kamala Harris—
the first woman, African American, and Asian American in that position—
presided over the Senate vote to confirm Jackson's nomination,
she penned a note to her goddaughter.

"I sit here with a deep sense of pride and joy—
for this moment in our history and what I believe
it will mean for you and all the current
young and future leaders of our country."

The next day, on the White House lawn, the president, the vice president, and the newly confirmed nominee celebrated the victorious vote. President Biden introduced the then-soon-to-be associate justice. "In America," he said, "everyone should be able to go as far as their hard work and God-given talent will take them."

Then, Ketanji Brown Jackson rose.

Quoting Maya Angelou's famous poem "Still I Rise," she framed the long journey to justice.

"It has taken 232 years and 115 prior appointments for a Black woman to be selected to serve on the Supreme Court of the United States.
But we've made it.
We've made it, all of us."

For every brown-skinned girl and every Black woman
who was ever overlooked or underestimated when
opportunities were doled out,
Ketanji Brown Jackson rose.

Constance
Baker Motley

Shirley Chisholm

Mae Jemison

Maya Angelou

"I am standing on the shoulders of my own role models.
And our children are telling me that they see now,
more than ever, that, here in America, anything is possible."

On June 30, 2022, with her husband and daughters present, Ketanji Brown Jackson rose to take her oaths.

For President Biden, her swearing in signaled a new dawn. Ketanji Brown Jackson's rise "to the highest court in the land," he said, "makes the sun shine on so many of us in a new way."

Though just shy of five feet, Ketanji Brown Jackson
stands tall among American jurists
and is herself a role model for children everywhere.

A Letter to My Granddaughter and All of Our Daughters

*D*ear Cara,

In the early 1980s, before your mother was born, I worked for the National Bar Association in Washington, D.C. I got to meet the Black lawyers behind important causes and historic cases:

Elaine Jones, the first woman to serve as director-counsel of the NAACP Legal Defense Fund (LDF);

Fred Gray, who represented Rosa Parks during the Montgomery Bus Boycott; and

Jane Bolin, who in 1939 became the first—and was for twenty years the only—Black female judge.

Thurgood Marshall, a leading civil rights lawyer and the first Black associate justice, was still on the Supreme Court then. I sat in the chambers as cases were heard.

In the 1980s, I did not dream of a Black woman on the highest court of the land. But in 2022, President Joe Biden announced the historic nomination with two brilliant Black women at his side—Vice President Kamala Harris and Judge Ketanji Brown Jackson. That picture sent a powerful message: Black women had a seat at the table.

The long overdue appointment confirmed what Black women had always known: We belong. I could not help but cry.

There are still obstacles to overcome, doors to open, and hills to climb. Draw on the hope and strength of your ancestors. Your place is in the sun.

Shine!

Beeps/ C B Weatherford

★ Ketanji Brown Jackson Timeline ★

- **1968:** April 4, the Reverend Martin Luther King, Jr., is assassinated in Memphis, Tennessee.

- **1970:** September 14, Ketanji Onyika Brown is born in Washington, D.C., to Johnny and Ellery Brown.
  Brown family relocates to Florida, where Johnny attends University of Miami School of Law.

- **1979:** Brother, Ketajh, is born.

- **1988:** Graduates from Miami Palmetto Senior High School, where she was class president and a star debater.
  Enters Harvard University, where she studies government.

- **1992:** Graduates with honors from Harvard University and works as a reporter for *Time* magazine.

- **1994:** Enters Harvard Law School, where she serves as an editor of the *Harvard Law Review*.

- **1996:** Graduates with honors from Harvard Law School.
  Marries surgeon Patrick Jackson.

- **1996–98:** Clerks for two federal judges.

- **1998:** Joins a law firm in Washington, D.C.

- **1999:** Clerks for U.S. Supreme Court Associate Justice Stephen Breyer.

- **2000:** Joins a law firm in Boston.
  Gives birth to daughter Talia.

- **2002:** Joins a law firm in Washington, D.C.

- **2003:** Is named assistant special counsel to the U.S. Sentencing Commission, a bipartisan agency that develops federal sentencing policy.

- **2004:** Gives birth to daughter Leila.

- **2005:** Serves as federal public defender in Washington, D.C.

- **2007:** Joins a law firm in Washington, D.C.

- **2008:** Barack Obama is elected as the first Black president of the United States.

- **2009:** Nominated by President Obama as vice chair of the U.S. Sentencing Commission. A bipartisan vote by the U.S. Senate confirms her in 2010.

- **2012:** Nominated by President Obama to be a judge for the U.S. District Court for the District of Columbia. There is no Senate vote.

- **2013:** Nominated again to the U.S. District Court for the District of Columbia. Two months later, the U.S. Senate votes to confirm the appointment.

- **2021:** Nominated by President Joe Biden and is confirmed to serve on the U.S. Court of Appeals for the D.C. Circuit.

- **2022:** Nominated by President Biden to replace Justice Breyer on the U.S. Supreme Court.